Fortitude

Chantelle Lowe

Fortitude

Anthology – Volume Four

Chantelle Lowe

All rights reserved. No part of this book may be reproduced or transmitted in any form or by any means, electronic or mechanical, including photocopying, recording, or by any information storage and retrieval system, without permission in writing from the publisher.

Published by Chantelle Griffin, originally known as Chantelle Lowe, in 2025

Interior layout by Chantelle Lowe

Cover artwork by Chantelle Lowe

Photograph: Fossil Island

Catalogue-in-Publication details available from the National Library of Australia

paperback ISBN: 978-0-6455661-2-3

Also available in hardback
ISBN: 978-0-6455661-3-0

Copyright © Chantelle Griffin, originally known as Chantelle Lowe, 2025

All rights reserved. No part of this book may be reproduced or transmitted in any form or by any means, electronic or mechanical, including photocopying, recording, or by any information storage and retrieval system, without permission in writing from the author.

Dedication

In memory of the author, John Bryson, who dedicated the time and experience to write one of the most important stories in Australian history. His words have been reassuring throughout the struggle that followed.

Contents

Fortitude

Accepting	1
Across the sea	2
Across the shadows	3
A distant reminder	6
A fragile movement	7
After it begins	8
Against appreciation	9
Against the current	10
Alone	13
An eternal question	14
Anew	15
A perpetual reminder	16

A shallow memory	17
A turbulent page unread	19
Be another	22
Be assertive	24
Beyond sight	25
Blackbirds	26
Blurred	27
By night	29
Calm between madness	30
Catching memories	31
Challenging tide	32
Circling the line	33
Claim of war	35
Clay	38
Complex combination	39
Continuance	40
Continuous reminder	41
Contrast of discretion	43
Counterfeit	44
Cover the soul	46
Creeping wind	47
Darkest dawn	48
Daunting predicament	49
Determination rising	51

Disarray in motion	52
Discover the whole	53
Disingenuous	54
Doors of time	55
Down into despair	56
Eclipse	57
Edges that permeate	58
Emptiness remains	61
Enough to know	62
Eternal creases	63
Eternal flame of courage	64
Ever changing	66
Ever reaching moments	67
Everything comes back	68
Faded despair	69
Fading in the waves	70
Fading into despair	73
Fading power	74
Fading shadows	75
Faint moments	76
Falling	79
Filled moments	80
Find myself	81
Flow of uncertainty	82

Framing the idea	83
From the setting sun	84
Grasping	85
Grasping onto something	86
Greater	87
Grieving the past	89
Happened then	90
Hard truth	91
Haunting sound	92
Hazy afternoon	93
Hint	94
Hollow day	95
Hollows of time	97
Hope held aloft	98
Hopeless belief	99
Hopelessness	100
Horror	101
If thoughts held meaning	102
Informed	103
In its place	105
In perpetuity	106
Integral decay	107
In the shadows of time	108
Into frustration	110

Into the world	111
Intrepid loneliness	112
Jealousy	113
Keep it so	114
Know not when	115
Lamp	116
Lasting game	117
Leaves of time	118
Leaving	119
Left there to find	120
Left unclaimed	122
Left unfound	125
Lonely gathering	126
Lone traveller	128
Long held past	130
Lost dreams evermore	132
Lost to begin with	134
Memories in solace	135
Mixed dreams	137
Mortal wound	138
Moving remnants	140
Narrow night	141
No in between	142
No mark	143

No more the dark carries	144
No patience	147
Not knowing	148
Obelisk	149
Oblivion	150
On a small dream	151
One desire	152
One journey to trace	153
One person	154
One small act	155
On my own	157
On the wave of regret	158
Other self	159
Our mistakes	160
Over the landscape	161
Paralleled sadness	162
Passing through	163
Path of intuition	165
Path of tragedy	166
Piling in a mound	167
Predicament	168
Pressure	169
Presumptuous dream	170
Prism of uncertainty	173

Quandary	174
Reaping madness	175
Redeeming factor	176
Reeling	177
Rejection	179
Remnant for which I mourn	180
Replacement	182
Rhythmless tide	183
Rippling away	184
Rising from burden	185
Roads that intertwine	186
Rupturing the flow	187
Rustling leaves	188
Sadness overwhelmed	189
Same place	190
Seek and find	192
Shallow fall	193
Shall strike	194
Sharpness felt	195
Shell of time	196
Shoulder of time	197
Slumber	198
Solace with intention	201
Solid page	202

Something heard	203
Something surreal	204
Sorrows underneath	206
Soul searching	207
Still I do not see	209
Stop them	210
Strength to stand	212
Sweeping past	214
Take away the harm	215
Taking hold	216
Tangled in the fray	217
Task of ambition	219
Tethered breeze	220
The concept of the legacy	221
The concept of the mark	222
The coming of night	223
The day flourishes	225
The deepest thoughts	226
The idea lingers	228
The mind that is	229
The path of integrity	231
The path that leads	234
The path turned	235
The real me	236

The unresolved	237
Through the essence	240
Tied with destiny	241
Time draped in harshness	242
Time of disbelief	245
Time to regret	246
To be without	247
To imagination	248
To know	249
Toll of integrity	250
To ruin	251
Tragedy unravels	252
Trapped in betrayal	253
Travesty	255
Treachery seeping through	256
Troubled path	258
Unacceptance	259
Uncommon means	260
Undefined layer	261
Underlying fold	262
Underneath the strain	264
Uneasiness	266
Unhelpful wish	267
Unintentional remnants	268

Unknown quantity	269
Unmarked terrain	270
Untimely thought	271
Waiting patiently	273
War	274
Way assured	276
Way we fall	277
What has been wrought	278
When darkness calls	279
When no one hears	280
When sadness reappears	282
When the final hand moves	284
Where others fear	286
Where reasons fade	287
Whirling in a storm	288
Whirling time	291
Would it shatter?	292
Wretchedness	293
Writhing in the moment	294
Yet to be remedied	295
Your shoulders	296
Your turn	297

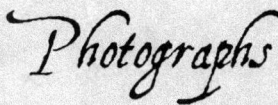

Photographs of Fossil Island, 28 December 2022

12	96	208
18	104	218
23	124	224
28	129	230
34	136	244
42	146	254
50	156	263
60	164	272
72	172	281
78	178	290
88	200	

Acknowledgements

I would like to thank Greg Lowe and Sally Shaw for their encouragement.

Foreward

One last moment of hesitation then it was all over, one last moment turning back toward the house that had been full of so many dreams, one last moment to remember how it had fallen apart. My possessions were packed to the top of the seats in the car but it did not matter, soon the house would be sold but it did not matter, my life had changed but none of that mattered. Chronic fatigue had taken many things, but somehow I would start again.

Chantelle Lowe

Accepting

Confrontation of who I am.
Acceptance of reality,
accepting who I really am.
What is it you say,
what have I done?
I recognise who I am.

Chantelle Lowe

Across the sea

I fathom the stars,
across the sea,
to churn amongst my mist.

Chantelle Lowe

Across the shadows

For not all can follow the path ahead,
when the day breaks anew to set the sky,
fleeting across the shadows hidden instead,
to prey upon the fragile that go by.

An anguish mixed with sadness bid to rest,
when the ashes grow cold from the delay,
yet the only offer is low at best,
when sifting through the timing that holds sway.

To grant the final tally at the end,
with a certainty mired in regret,
taking hold in the middle to defend,
the sorrows that drench into plans unset.

For the path ahead is filled with intent,
washing away internal hopes that fade,

Chantelle Lowe

pulled in a relentless game of descent,
ebbing closer to the edge of the blade.

Where turmoil lurks from the corners out,
to saturate the remnants to dispense,
in the aftermath of silence and doubt,
where the only path creates no defence.

All while the past stays front of stage,
to linger in the folds of time with deceit,
churning in the unrest of ev'ry page,
where the lost moment echoes in defeat.

For the passage that slips away from all,
may call again to bring the resting hand,
immersing in the fateful light to fall,
grappling with the remaining place to stand.

On the virtue that plagues all known to reason,
with the emptiness that hollows the mind,
when the darkness surmounts to find treason,
where the vulnerable were left behind.

Seeking a way through the turmoil cast,

Chantelle Lowe

amid the array of all that was said,
to remain in the strength to hold out last,
with a resolve that sought the path ahead.

Chantelle Lowe

A distant reminder

A choice,
a single choice,
a strength in recognition.
A reminder,
a late reminder,
of a distant memory.
A place,
a lasting place,
a recognition the same.
Yet in all this,
one thing changed.
A line,
a tumultuous line,
very well refined.

A fragile movement

A fledgling mortal wound in hand,
takes swift refuge in my company,
making hope within the sand,
that washes away before me.

A fragile movement before the shore,
sways with the breeze trickling past,
leaving no path as it was before,
with every thought fading fast.

A whisper calling as the waves rush in,
slowing streams over tiny shells,
caressing each moment from within,
as all that was gives and tells.

A time when hope was far away,
yet fleeting past it did not stay.

After it begins

What is time when time is eternal?
It plagues on the soul,
the eternal message giving rise to space,
a point of imagination and uncertainty.
Caressing the body back and forth,
lulling it into a false sense of security,
not knowing which way is meant to be.
When time called on it for a purpose,
and that purpose is yet to be found.
Come with me on that journey,
and follow me as I go.
Where I end up is not known,
somehow the journey starts after it begins,
a false move, then the real one after.
Making no sense when it happens.

Chantelle Lowe

Against appreciation

To discriminate,
against appreciation,
of the unknown.
Is forever,
an underlying surface.

Chantelle Lowe

Against the current

Turmoil swims in the waters deep,
taking a while to move and creep,
toppling through the unwanted streets,
and the many unheard defeats.

Spiralling against the current,
in the ever raging torrent,
filling the waterways ahead,
with all the underlying dread.

Yet rising forth in calm of ease,
slithered the unresolved to tease,
trudging into the open fray,
wiping the hopes and dreams away.

Striking certainty where it stood,
hidden among the dense laid wood,

Chantelle Lowe

for time is a healer unbound,
when no one is left to be found.

Chantelle Lowe

Alone

To be,
to be none,
to be one.
I alone, and I alone shall see.

Chantelle Lowe

An eternal question

Confusion, desperation drenching the figure that stands,
in a glimpse that saturates the world in an image,
moving with an elaborate speed that carries forth,
and all the while the original is lost.

Lost to the turmoil that made the initial demands,
that covered the folds of time underneath the damage,
unfurling the distraction in uncertainty henceforth,
to concentrate the eternal question within the cost.

Anew

I have changed,
I have become a new.
Why do I look to my past,
when I have entered a new phase in my life?
I have come so far,
yet I have such a way left.
Please guide me,
please give me strength.
I need all the help I can get.

Chantelle Lowe

A perpetual reminder

It is with a settled mind that time greets me,
the sadness grows with the happiness that endures,
a perpetual reminder of the past that sets free,
calling out as the intrepid memory lures.

A place holding the resolute in turmoil,
where all struggles cease in rapid succession,
grasping the upheaval through the toil,
to clasp the ever resulting fusion.

If time stood still it would hold a shattered life,
yet its passing strengthens with every stride,
wiping away the anguish with the strife,
as the travelled coarse path grows wide.

A moment of regret washed away with the tears,
fading with it all the troubles and fears.

Chantelle Lowe

A shallow memory

There is no end in sight above the marching haze,
for time seeps through the eternal pattern,
passing by the landscape with a traveller's gaze,
a lasting vision without knowing when to return.

For the day stands still with a pleasant ease,
after the winds of turmoil seep in,
taking with it the crippling breeze,
rising from the shadow's untimely din.

A place where the sun warms the land,
echoing the reaches with each passing light,
caressing the solitary final demand,
as all nears the last journey into the night.

A shallow memory swept through the chill air,
as the price of life came down to bear.

Chantelle Lowe

A turbulent page unread

To despair disparity,
in the evolving light.
To try to remedy,
with all my might.
To close a door,
unhinged and worn.
To seek out more,
when the day is torn.
To move against the fray,
when the tide is done.
To call out the way,
when there is only one.
To trail the source,
as the shadow fades.
With no other recourse,
when the time abrades.
To sway across the breeze,

Chantelle Lowe

when all matters hold tight.
To the rolling sense of unease,
remaining out of sight.
To wash away the memory,
of a moment time forgot.
Coursing through the tragedy,
of an intertwined knot.
To make my way ahead,
when there is little doubt.
To rush against the tide instead,
and left to figure out.
For all that has come ashore,
no tidings does it bring.
Across the way as before,
in weathered hollow ring.
No place holds true,
amid the path long sought,
for only sorrow grew,
where the timeless gage was caught.
A turbulent page unread,
when the day grew all too long.
With many words left unsaid,
within a mind that held strong.
For I have come here,

Chantelle Lowe

crossing paths untold.
Not out of whim or fear,
to watch the way unfold.

Be another

I will always be another,
and I know in time will become greater,
aspects of virtuality,
in my reposed response,
to another.
In greater conflict or need,
as one we rise,
to always be beaten in some way,
however not all,
to be consumed,
in this way,
of ever yonder.

Be assertive

One life, live it, one life, struggling to be.
One life, take it, use it,
be it.
Be higher, be better, be surer,
be assertive.
Be ruthless at getting what you aim for,
be generous to those who give it.

Chantelle Lowe

Beyond sight

To see beyond sight,
is an enormity,
beyond light,
of what has been.

Blackbirds

Placid is the day ahead with all its glorious rays,
warming the ground beneath my feet,
in simple and reminding ways,
caressing the wind with a steady heat.

For upon the air chirps a merry song,
from gathering in the open shade,
announcing their delight to belong,
where the garden skinks parade.

Blurred

Mind blurred.
...Absent, absent, absent.
Darkness calls,
reaching out.
...Think, think, think.
Falling into a numb swirling
of never ending unconsciousness.
...Slowly, slowly, slowly.
Trapped, cannot get out.
...Try, try, try.

Chantelle Lowe

By night

I come,
I go by night.
Away from resourcefulness,
and into confusion.

Chantelle Lowe

Calm between madness

Intrepid is the friend that sits by my side,
comforting me in days of folly and sadness,
for the way ahead is sometimes marred.
Consumed by the ever reaching tide,
bringing a calm in between the madness,
as a friendship ensures the chaos is barred.

Chantelle Lowe

Catching memories

Placard of richness, it sees the lies,
it sees through me.
It sees through the past,
it catches the memories one by one.
I am the bearer of truth,
the bearer of reality.

Chantelle Lowe

Challenging tide

The challenge that befalls the rising tide,
is one that does not diminish,
catering for the various whims.

Circling the line

Tragedy strikes the cruellest of fate,
tipping the scales accrued in the wake,
travelling down with the wholly innate,
circling the line between all that is fake.

Chantelle Lowe

Claim of war

When comes a night of shimmering grey upon the light,
shall shine on the flowing dark scales,
the fire of many a star.
Thus will rain the blood draining,
from many fallen into everlasting sleep.
Upward will rise the lifeless creatures,
taking back the land which once was peaceful.
Dawn shall break many a year later,
and there will lie a field of evergreen.

In the blazing hot rage of fire,
which seeped along the surface,
flung like rain from the deep caverns light,
came the scowl of many,
who had vowed to devastate,
that which was not theirs.
Voices, oh many voices,

Chantelle Lowe

like the screech of an angered bird,
barely audible over the flames' hunger.
Then, just the swooping of strong,
flightful wings, heard slowly,
like an unsteady heartbeat filling the sky's night,
and the rosy red oven below.
When it came for the sphere of white gold to waken,
slightly,
the black of the once settled earth,
showed vast in the rays of light,
and the vowed souls revealed,
hung silent.

As he looked he saw nothing except the peace it held,
the rhythmic sounds of the ocean faraway.
The intensity of the landscape,
now it was theirs,
to settle and establish.
All were steadily united in their labour and effort,
nothing to stop their triumph,
their monotonous victory.
Forever it would last,
and they would rise,
in the peace,

Chantelle Lowe

in their place.
Never to be upheld,
never to be disturbed by another unity,
for never would another be established,
ever.

Chantelle Lowe

Clay

Into the fire I see the mud,
all dark stricken and dry,
the multitude that played with it,
are now gone by.

Complex combination

I stand alone,
I am special in every way.
I am not what was before,
but a complex combination,
made up from hate and love,
from destruction and removal,
from instability.
A force unreckoned with,
a strength untold.
Making my own path,
where there was none.
Not even the best have gone before,
and the worst are left far behind,
in what is reality.

Chantelle Lowe

Continuance

I look at the past,
to see the present,
and find the future.

Chantelle Lowe

Continuous reminder

A dream, a mission, a sole desire,
an intense and ritual pact.
A realisation springing forth,
from the depths below.
An urgence, timely and forgotten,
bending to the wielding blow.
Time is no stranger here,
making its presence felt.
As someone more mature emerges,
from the lineal, androgynous belt.
I am the seer, the planner,
the ever-continuous reminder,
that art is everywhere.

Chantelle Lowe

Contrast of discretion

Intrepidation,
a figment of imagination,
a termination of a lie.
Revelation,
in contrast of discretion,
in recollection gone by.
Situation,
upon reflection of a time,
in desecration intended to rely.
Culmination,
in transgression faded,
of an undue transference to untie.

Counterfeit

Interior to menace, counterfeit to menace,
to contribute to my own,
is in say,
of a whole,
though never,
is a long time.
To dwindle,
in the approximate,
of another's theme,
in destiny's eye,
all hold back,
from a time.
In the diabolical of circumference,
of an enemies gate,
to open in distil,
where haste less and ponder more,
to the accompany,

Chantelle Lowe

as an assailant,
may upon us muse,
the intellectual.

Chantelle Lowe

Cover the soul

A time and place covers my soul,
it touches the ground and envelopes the corners of my sight.
I had it in the form, a nurtured whole,
it was not the way, I had to fight.
Playing games with the torturous,
in a calm and ebbing combination.

Chantelle Lowe

Creeping wind

Eating the metal, eating the concrete,
it thrives on wearing down.
'I am the wind,' it says,
and I hear its mighty roar.
It's cold inside,
in the bottom of my heart.
It creeps through the layers of my skin,
and finds me there,
all calm and quiet.

Chantelle Lowe

Darkest dawn

A way ahead foreshadows the darkest dawn,
trailing into the open wind swept sky,
for not long shall I go into the morn'.

Daunting predicament

A dynasty of tragedy held up in the hand,
a cornerstone of empathy lost upon the edge,
to hold in disarray a deceit throughout the land,
where callers made their way towards the ledge.

An uncertainty struck deep into the fraying mind,
a restitution yet unfelt troubling every moment,
to trail a path truly difficult to find,
when rests the daunting predicament.

Preceding the inevitable timing of uncertainty,
in a fragile and discouraging thought,
filtering an uneven form of reality,
breaking the surface of what has been brought.

In a glimpse of indeterminate discretion,
founded on the verge of retribution.

Determination rising

The intrepid follower through the moments of time,
reminiscing along the path as it winds away,
crossing the steep foreboding mountains yet to climb,
left in the passing memory of yesterday.

Tracing every step and holding back regret,
in the midst of the building raging storm,
where it would be easier to fall back and forget,
as all the moments culminate to take form.

Nowhere along the journey was there pause,
to wallow in the overwhelming thought,
yet all the actions braced against the cause,
from a determination in the moment sought.

For no tragedy greater is struck upon the will,
when abandoned there is no more love to instil.

Disarray in motion

Tragedy strikes under the ultimate frames,
giving way to the desperate in meaning,
when the gaze upon a solace that renames,
in the burden strips away all knowing.

From the disaster that dwells in the placid mind,
beckoning to rummage through the forgotten past,
reassembled into the vastness left behind,
in the determination created to last.

An intensity flowing through reassurance,
when the faint line from existence to the end,
of the sojourn that follows the ultimate stance,
embedded in the raging sorrows that amend.

When all the shadows gather dust through emotion,
carrying forward the disarray in motion.

Chantelle Lowe

Discover the whole

Discover, discover, discover the whole,
of which I am part.
Break free of the mould,
and become something great.

Disingenuous

A transition remains to aspire to the long awaited moment,
held in a masterful art encapsulated on the floor,
interpreted in the disingenuous portrayal to lament,
when the verge mortifies the inconsequential forever more.

Chantelle Lowe

Doors of time

Windows opening the doors of time,
and I peer in.
What do I find when all is lost,
and I could not see?
I opened the door to find an end,
I opened it to see 'round the bend.
In a way I already knew what to find,
I already knew the way in kind.
Another person in a puzzle filled with dread,
found the little body already dead,
and in a flutter of time on the floor,
here this memory shall rest evermore.

Down into despair

Down, down into intellect and retrospect,
down, down into despair and the timeless snare,
down, down below the surface of the preface.
Down, down to the melancholy and wanton folly,
down, down the impunity of indiscretion,
down, down the careless hand upon the land.
For as we go no creature spent will time relent.

Chantelle Lowe

Eclipse

A destiny that casts a shadow with a fading light,
transitioning into an eclipse to purge the nightmare,
that creeps into the day long after the final insight,
flowing from the shadows that pass into a distant stare.

Chantelle Lowe

Edges that permeate

An ebbing weight fluctuates with the resonation of time,
overlapping the inevitable in the culmination of the mind,
sweeping away the detection of an everlasting crime,
where certainty sways in the balance of those who find.

A recognition above all others in the eternity of space,
granting reason where there is none at the trail's end,
marking the many paths ahead down the final chase,
where all that matters is left behind to descend.

Reaching out to the silence carried in the masterful patience,
as the ebbing flow caresses the edges that permeate,
through the thoughts that meld into the conscience,
leaving traces from the myriad of decisions that deviate.

Culminating in the eternal picture that constantly fades,
into the darkest rendition of thoughts and fears,

Chantelle Lowe

overflowing into timelessness formed by many barricades,
swirling along the edges as the memory of the past disappears.

Placing the unwinding trail into the faded hour,
as consequences left undone seep into the distant fray,
unreconciled amid the harm that could devour,
when the movement of the last intention calls away.

Emptiness remains

Tragedy surpasses the time that flies into the breeze,
an ever quivering temptation filled with vacancy,
the eminent reprieve that takes over with ease,
when the last moment of trouble passes into the sea.

A covering of the soul in intrepidation,
as the unwavering solace washes away,
seeping through the sadness held in volition,
reaching the path as it dives through the fray.

For time it holds the epitome of them all,
upon the surface at the glimpse of dusk,
when the emptiness remains after the fall,
and the shell once whole, crushes to a husk.

In the wind that blows a memory,
and all the while it was let to fall free.

Chantelle Lowe

Enough to know

Opening a window onto the past,
do I dare to see it?
It was failing in the wind,
blowing in every path.
I knew it but for a little while,
and that was enough to know,
That this was something special,
something with a warming glow.

Chantelle Lowe

Eternal creases

The eternal flow creases behind the uneven door,
calling for restitution when hope is lost,
a turmoil bringing with it a silence before,
the final requisite exposed the true cost.

Chantelle Lowe

Eternal flame of courage

Tragedy infernal,
a culmination of fear,
placed on a trigger,
when all take care.
No doubt upon the steady hand,
reaching from without.
For no one stood before,
and yet again,
in another way.
Calling into repetition,
a cold uncertainty,
a harsh reminder,
peering down.
Resting darkness and insincerity,
a long strand played so fine,
a trigger on a tether,
twining on a line.

Chantelle Lowe

A brazen moment,
yet unmatched,
with contingency.
A callousness unrepentant,
sweeping through with haste,
a spoken word left unsaid,
when the damage is left to waste.
An unparalleled consequence,
of an unknown timing,
laid a moment unprofound.
A devastation in a fraction,
covering the time unread,
and no empathy in sight.
For travelling the faded path,
of a long held memory,
a time when strength held,
from past tragedy.
A moment long forgotten,
as the tide did turn,
an eternal flame of courage,
that will live and burn.

Chantelle Lowe

Ever changing

I am winter,
I am the storm,
I am the overlapping form.
Constant,
ever changing,
embedding itself into infinity.

Chantelle Lowe

Ever reaching moments

Treasure the moments that rise and fall,
with the ever reaching tide as it flows,
whispering along the breeze for one and all it goes.

Chantelle Lowe

Everything comes back

Try as all you might to break free,
everything comes back in the dark to plague the mind.
Terrible lies amongst all the anger,
a harsh way to travel behind.
A feeling once said forgotten,
taking away the breath of every person.
Just for a moment lost in the pattern,
facing the timeless image undone.

Faded despair

A tumultuous mess is left in the ravenous mind,
taken in by a residing quandary,
an elegant map with the design to bind,
in the hidden moments of lost glory.
For the way ahead will shatter all,
when an erroneous passage does befall.

An untimely movement left to recoil,
in the darkness of a faded despair,
a tragedy wrapped in the daily toil,
of an undesired intrusion meant to tear.
When one decision leads down the solitary lane,
gathering with it all those who remain.

Chantelle Lowe

Fading in the waves

The path to intrepidation warrants the pounding sorrow that glides within,
and returns a level of uncertainty when time crashes in,
culminating in the disguise of heroism embodied in the fading waves,
capturing the essence of the final lines drawn as the way forward paves.

Long have I seen the last of the dying ways in the fleeting past,
reaching out for those who grasp onto the shadows cast,
with the embers scattering on the whims of a swirling reality,
moving forward in the space of the wise who will let the thing be.

Places shift in the sand of many fading trails,
washed away with the hopes in many unruly gales,
leaving the ebb and flow of faded memories stirring behind,
reconciling with the entities reaching out to find.

For the way ahead may be grim in the early days that remain,
tilting the turmoil unsaid weathering the storm of loss or gain,

Chantelle Lowe

a tragedy unfurled as the tide draws near to wash away,
the sadness drenching the ground in the thought of come what may.

Fading into despair

In the darkness of all that is right, the terrible truth comes out,
no shame, no guilt, stays wrapped around me.
From the time I was so small,
it centres itself around me, waiting for the call.
But what do I seek when I am not there,
or do I seek at all?
Is this the way it was meant to be,
when nobody said at all?
I seek, I hide, I do not find what is below,
for it slowly creeps its way up my soul, fading into despair.
Not knowing which way to run and flee,
when everything seems too much.
It takes courage to stand up, it takes courage to let go,
it takes courage to move forward and be yourself.

Chantelle Lowe

Fading power

The eternal consumption of rarity devours with every page,
a risk of all uncertainty in light of the day's late hour,
a transfixed array through the ending of the age,
when the last wisps break away with the fading power.

An untold deniability wraps around the swirling edge,
an unfortunate disarray to the unkept final word,
for the might to follow to the very end of the pledge,
before the unseen rise forward to be heard.

If time's dark eternal grace seeps into view,
the last whispers will devour and bleed through.

Chantelle Lowe

Fading shadows

The paradigm of eternity sits upon a precipice,
while the world goes travelling by,
a tangible moment resting on the edifice,
rising through the grime to reach the sky.

Stalling the conclusion of the inevitable,
colliding with the fading shadows,
fleeting on a whim of what would be possible,
winding along the trailing breeze that follows.

Gathering clouds flock in the falling day,
intensifying where once the sun did shine,
creeping in as the shadows come to stay,
and all the while waiting to align.

For as the darkness sweeps the land,
so shall the sky make its final demand.

Chantelle Lowe

Faint moments

Pieces of a picture fall to the ground,
if I hadn't touched it then it wouldn't be around,
fluttering through the wind swept air,
tumbling in motion without a care.

Tumultuous rearranging in an endless flame,
shedding all guilt in an unbrought blame,
whirling to the end of a sentence,
where all is wrapped up in pretence.

A time away held in solitude,
grasping a faint moment to elude,
when all is lost but known,
amid the pieces that have blown.

Scattered far to find another day,
floating along a path before they stay,

Chantelle Lowe

pieces of a memory flying through the wind,
until the healing of time does rescind.

For may the journey find an end,
far from the way around the bend,
and stray not far from the mortal eye,
calling faintly as the seasons go by.

Falling

With every step the hour grows longer,
seeping into the ever gleaming day,
whiling away the time ever stronger,
with the flittering breeze coming to stay.

If time was not fading with every thought,
it would wait in the brilliant light,
for the calming moment brought,
as every sound falls with all its might.

A tragedy held as the sun goes past,
falling lower still with every creature,
taking in the sky until the shadows cast,
stirring as time brings forth its treasure.

For every moment brings anew,
a calling of a path so true.

Filled moments

For all the sequences that lay before,
for all the restless unease that follows,
for all the winding paths upon the shore,
for all the moments filled with sorrows.

For I have played upon the sand of time,
with every weary step laid bare,
taking the weight of a steady climb,
through the memories carrying despair.

For a terrible moment that lay ahead,
sifting through the unseen blame,
wallowing along the paths unsaid,
filled with life's eternal flame.

For the cherished memories that remain,
there carries the cost in light of the gain.

Chantelle Lowe

Find myself

Responding to misinterpretations of a life unsaid,
isolating me before I had a chance to grow.
I was crippled into something other than myself,
and that is the person they saw,
that is the person they knew.
It was a person that was made up by
someone other than myself.
Something worth almost nothing,
and then that destructive influence was taken away,
and I was left with no knowledge of who I was.
A small figure with no self identity,
and no self worth.
From this I had to find the one person that mattered the most,
myself.

Chantelle Lowe

Flow of uncertainty

The depth of pain which grasps the problem disintegrates,
and the whole enormity of the situation flows into uncertainty.
The truth of the matter taking effect in voluptuous tirades,
into the isolating turmoil covering the soul covered with empathy.

It is truly condemning to see such accolades given in ignorance,
yet the soul weeps ever longer for the mark of hope,
Curling up through the framework giving a small chance,
in a world that seems so dim and it is enough just to cope.

I do not see your smile, for you only show me pain,
a translucent hatred vexing the whole of your face.
A rigid harsh reality focusing on the ambitions of gain,
forgetting what it is to live and care in this place.

In the ray of triumph the silhouette of trust is extinguished,
and no amount of frantic rambling can have it replenished.

Chantelle Lowe

Framing the idea

Colouring the mind,
colouring the space in time,
colouring opposition,
colouring the naked decision.
Framing, making, taking, forsaking,
pilfering the idea.
Tragic or so it seems, it can be real,
taken from prior thoughts,
lifted to satisfy other rorts.

From the setting sun

Shadows grow where time dwells in sorrow,
far reaching across the wind swept land,
towering over those who wish to borrow,
with a searing toll in a final demand.

If it were not the way to step forward,
when the fear grows weak in the distance,
to reconcile and move toward,
the divide that wakens from a trance.

To quell the woes that haunt from the past,
and drench the rains that fell in disgrace,
with the burden of time to the way cast,
when the sorrows that drain are put into place.

Not long will I travel with what has begun,
resting into the shadows from the setting sun.

Chantelle Lowe

Grasping

Oh my,
where do I sit?
All day,
grasping the pen,
of truth.

Chantelle Lowe

Grasping onto something

Without questioning one is like the other,
both grasping onto something which is not.
Take away everything which has become false,
what is left is harsh, sharp, and true.
Containing the pure essence which exists.

Chantelle Lowe

Greater

Why is this the way it has to be,
I wanted to be something,
greater than what I am?
What is it you know that I don't.
Get rid of this feeling inside my head,
make it go away.
I just want to die,
I want to get rid of this feeling.
Take it away.
I just want to be me.

Chantelle Lowe

Grieving the past

Grieve past the rain, past the confusion,
grieve after the pain, after the fact,
grieve from the seeing, from knowing,
grieve after the fact.
Grieving long after the time is past,
grieving after the fact.
Grieving from knowing the damage that was done,
grieving after the harm that took place.
Grieving from dealing with the aftermath,
grieving from having the memories,
nasty memories which took place.
A disturbing foundation to lay upon,
one with no concept of pride,
one with no concept of self worth.

Happened then

To kill a life,
and hold the knife,
is something all too soon.
To bid goodbye,
and see you nigh,
will reap the caller's doom.
But I who see,
the worth in me,
will stay to rise again.
With all who knew,
the timing due,
in the event that happened then.

Chantelle Lowe

Hard truth

A time of attitudes,
a time of reconciliation.
I wish it was that,
but it is not.
I sometimes wish I could pretend a lie,
but I already know,
truth is hard as ice.

Haunting sound

In the final hour when the caller calls no more,
there lies the ability to slip past mortality,
a tragic repetition of the forces that deplore,
when all paths have overgrown in the memory.

A silence that hollows out the deepest haunting sound,
tracking a life back to a single moment,
in a glimpse of all the sorrow to be found,
and the darkest hours as all went.

The balance of eternity reaching a glimmer of calm,
passing through the unconscious mind,
seeping into a folly of resounding harm,
when all withers away with those lost behind.

For tragedy creeps through the mortal eye,
resting heavy as the years go by.

Chantelle Lowe

Hazy afternoon

Sweeping past the breeze of remembrance,
on a warm and hazy afternoon,
intricately played and left to chance.

Chantelle Lowe

Hint

I am thought, and reason too,
frolicking from hint or hand,
where others call and others stand.

Hollow day

Shattered is time,
gathered is mine.
Hollow is the day,
with the golden ray.

Chantelle Lowe

Hollows of time

Intrepid as the wind blows martyred in every way,
calling to the hollows of time webbing as it spins,
turning with the burning seasons on the bay,
for the traveller walks no more where the shore begins.

A furrowed brow that creases on the steady land,
an ageless gap of wisdom wrapped in eternity,
a frame of lasting presence marked upon the sand,
when steadier days lie ahead with integrity.

An eminent hand to guide on the unforeseen road,
where hope and dreams tread among the grass,
a distant memory unfolds and does forebode,
in a manner weaving widely through the pass.

If I were to hold my hand up perhaps I would catch it,
or feel an essence of familiar warmth remaining unlit.

Hope held aloft

If dreams sang upon a tethered page,
a hope long flown upon the breeze,
held fast aloft the mighty stage,
to clasp the unforeseen with ease.

Dare I might to trek along,
the fragile care of thought,
to glimpse upon the inner song,
that time before me brought.

Yet was this dream a tranquil deed,
or a turmoil sour to the edge,
for all the hopes it did feed,
held with one last pledge?

A dream that sang a little while,
and brought a brief but warming smile.

Chantelle Lowe

Hopeless belief

To see the other side,
and not turn back.
Would be hopeless,
beyond belief.

Hopelessness

As I fall upon the ground,
in midst of rumbling turmoil.
The heart is but an easy thing,
to portray a hope dismissed.
Into circles of the bound,
goes leaping in what we have found.
Caution, caution, to all within,
as losing loses everything.
Though may you hope to aspire,
in ground of gain,
because there is an undertow,
to drag the silent under.
In spread of hope and doom,
though none in gain will make haste.

Chantelle Lowe

Horror

Killer, killer,
comes and goes,
in the space, whole,
locked in time.
Did he see you,
standing there,
in horror,
and despair?
Such are these,
which I call,
for memories,
scarred and gone.

Chantelle Lowe

If thoughts held meaning

The plague of extended thoughts consumes,
in the fading hour of time,
a commiseration of all that pressures,
in the shadow of the sublime.

If travelled thoughts held meaning,
amidst the slowing of the day,
it would hold a moment grieving,
of a time held far away.

A memory seeping through the grace,
of the beaming sunlit rays,
hindering a silent long held pace,
hidden from the outside gaze.

An intrepidation held within the whole,
culminating upon the final toll.

Chantelle Lowe

Informed

In a small fragment,
the idea bursts forward,
presenting itself,
as an informed connection.

In its place

Therefore in its place, I shall hold
though I do not see
my ambitious thought.
Even if strong and clear it can be,
I often summon its greater power.
Though its dwindling one is far closer to me,
yet inside I feel I can never find it.
It hides, expecting me to pass it,
but I know, I can always find it.
If I wait
then it appears,
half knowingly, with its gentle smile
inside there, I find its warmth
and ever glowing glee.

In perpetuity

A skill, a time to hold a fine line,
captured in perpetuity in a sign,
that reveals the way marred ahead,
wrapping around eternity said.

For the writing that crashes the wall,
stagnates into an open pile,
rushing through the time spent to enthral,
fusing an elegance within style.

Where the hold of uncertainty takes,
through the concealment and rapture,
on the edge of empathy that brakes,
with the lost memories to capture.

In the prism of a space to let,
all aspirations fall in regret.

Chantelle Lowe

Integral decay

The interception of ideas in the integral of decay,
brings with it a troubled past covering the intrepid air.
For no sight I see which holds the passing of the day,
causing a reproach that trickled beyond repair.
So eminent was its fleeting glance, so near,
a fervent caller.

In the shadows of time

The tears that shatter are immense,
they glide down in a stream of uncertainty,
falling on the broken ground of a troubled woe,
amassing in the heart to dwell.
Yet fear not the time awaits,
slipping through the infinite mind,
pulling apart the last hold along the edge,
wrapping around the barriers entwined.
With a glimpse I can find the path I left behind,
in the shadows of time itself,
in the fading hour of the night close up,
when all is not forgotten in regret.
For once I led where echoes follow,
creating patterns in the floating dust,
carrying memories on a breeze without bounds,
ebbing into the distance with the fading light.
When time halts for but a moment,

Chantelle Lowe

when it captures what was lost,
sacrificing an eternal future for the past,
in a harshness that taunts in a fading dream.
When all the journeys lead to one,
and the time worth travelled remains undone.

Chantelle Lowe

Into frustration

Frustration, frustration and pure frustration,
not dealing with the situation,
not dealing with anything, not knowing.
Not wanting to withstand,
not knowing how.
No skills, except those of an aggressor.
Hidden under the layers of silence,
hidden under the lack of confidence,
hidden under the politeness.
The harshness left behind by a predator.
The harshness embedded in the soul.
A harshness and persistence that leaves the soul vacant.
A vacancy from what is left behind.
A vacancy in a mood,
a vacancy in a frame of mind.

Chantelle Lowe

Into the world

So far have I gone into the world,
that is not without hope of all,
who sees the figurative of time,
and knows that all has begun.

Intrepid loneliness

The problem with intrepid behaviour,
is the loneliness that follows.
When you get up and walk away,
from the cause of your problems.
The shadow creasing over my life,
which would not go its own way.
So instead I made my purpose known,
when I left all that behind.
I walked my own path from the door,
that held so much anguish and sadness.

Chantelle Lowe

Jealousy

Jealousy, jealousy,
comes and goes.
Jealousy,
the extravagant.

Chantelle Lowe

Keep it so

Is life such that I cannot see,
through all known benefactors,
to the tumbling turbulence below.
Behold, the reason why,
and keep it so.

Chantelle Lowe

Know not when

Time passes, onto merrier things.
It was a short and bitter time,
as we all do know it well.
Comes along a different time, yelling all too soon.
When all we wanted was to know,
that the little seed of knowledge,
sprung from so much past,
would fill the inspirations cast.
All the while this little vessel created on the waves,
ripples of impressions left behind in grace.
But do I really know the person from within,
when all is done, even though I knew not when.

Chantelle Lowe

Lamp

In the dead of night,
when I turned on the light,
nothing was left to stay.

Chantelle Lowe

Lasting game

For all shall see the mortal flare,
and I shall recoil in despair,
when there is no one left to blame,
in the shadow of the lasting game.

Chantelle Lowe

Leaves of time

Treacherous are the leaves of time,
flittering to the ground.
Sampling all that life has given,
only to be found.
Awaiting the last goodbye at every turn.

Chantelle Lowe

Leaving

I left the arm that held me,
I left the fire,
it chased me,
far away.

Chantelle Lowe

Left there to find

Transition to eternity.
The effervescence of peace,
taking form to exposition.
Derived from the consciousness,
of the real world flying past.
Taking away the true form.
Livid are the creatures,
reaching up from the sky.
A detrimental transition,
of frozen ice up high.
Calling, calling, I say forth,
for not of the premonition.
Filling, seeping through the way,
of the wish for that unobtained.
Trying, fleeting past the idea,
of a promineering transition.
Taking, holding, shaping forward,

Chantelle Lowe

taking time of as it may,
but in the distant future past,
can I find my way?
Taking, forfeiting,
the ever transitioning soul,
is it weeping for me to catch up,
in this ever busy world?
Transition, coalition,
do I find my way?
Is it there as it was before,
glimpsing from behind?
Take me away and find me again,
my ever burdened soul.
Did I take it?
Did I make it?
Do I see it flying past?
Transition, was it really real?
Opening up the mind,
taking out the many images
that I have there left to find.

Chantelle Lowe

Left unclaimed

The tide will turn on the weathered shore,
as all who have seen it went before,
chasing down the path of faded dreams,
lost in the running water of nearby streams.

Calling above the constant swaying trees,
in the ebb and flow of the dancing breeze,
if I speak above the rustling ground,
every word merges into the void of sound.

Seeping in with the unfolding day,
as the sunlight shifts along the bay,
carrying forward an unfinished goal,
in the glimpse of time it remains unwhole.

For the path is withered and left unsaid,
where hopes lay dashed and words unread,

Chantelle Lowe

the time calls me back again to see,
when all is lost and to let it be.

The moment worth knowing is left unmade,
to walk along underneath the shade,
where memories dance along a string,
until the wind leaves them scattering.

Yet all the while there is no breeze to find,
when the past settles in a state of mind,
and what lies barren is left unclaimed,
in the moment when we all are blamed.

Chantelle Lowe

Left unfound

Take the land which holds the earth,
keep it in the ground.
Let it grow and see the worth,
of a time that is left unfound.

Lonely gathering

A willingness to interrogate,
in a mire of suspicion,
when the road is lost,
and hope is held within.

An ability to investigate,
when the calls are dim,
setting through the key notes,
of a lonely gathering.

If not for long then when,
as the trail of turmoil fades,
a memory creeping past,
in all the forms and shades.

A tolerable intersection,
between the rising dust,

Chantelle Lowe

reminiscent in name,
within the faded rust.

A culmination of time,
sweeping away the tears,
in a bowl of optimism,
restricting all the fears.

Lone traveller

The peril that resists the change,
the passage to transition,
the integrity of the whole,
when the last that heals takes shape.
The underlying movement forward,
the reaching for the dawn,
the silence of passivity,
when the traveller takes a stride.
The malevolence of unheeded danger,
the fluidity of the tide,
the attribution to the soul,
when the life of one goes by.

Long held past

The rapture of progress takes us all into the dark,
with a precision that calls upon the greatest source,
perpetuating the endeavour along the mark,
when the fading hour brings no other course.

If I were to hold your hand and lead you away,
would you remember all that lies behind,
or hesitate in the moment and choose to stay,
when all that matters has been unkind?

Would you step forward when the path fades,
or would you fall into disarray?
When at every angle the past evades,
in all the memories that hold and sway.

Would I know you if we met after all is done,
when time finds a path to take its hold?

Chantelle Lowe

Where the whole travesty is left to none,
merging with travellers who have told.

For no longer does the burden last,
from a time captured in the long held past.

Lost dreams evermore

The sway of the breeze that takes away the pain,
the tragedy that wraps itself around the blame,
when all is lost on a whim that does not retain,
any cause for hope when the hold is the same.

The fall of the rain that draws the memory near,
the focus that stays in darkest shadows of despair,
in a culmination of frustration mingled in fear,
curled up in a desolate and solitary stare.

For the shadow that grows upon the shores of deceit,
lingers in the past all mired in the trenches of hurt,
in the edges of sorrow that deepens in the sign of defeat,
where the scars that follow remain hidden in the dirt.

No more shall the path tread deep in the distant past,
tarnishing the feelings that lay transparent on the floor,

Memories in solace

A constellation in the windows of the soul,
grappling to understand the incrimination,
that mercilessly procures the damage left whole,
with an unfettered grasp upon realisation.

Branching into the myriad of decisions,
laying claim to uncertainty when all are blind,
in a manner that seeps through perceptions,
lasting long into the dying night to remind.

In a parcel of time that waits from a distance,
disparagingly in the echoes that collate,
into a fractured image to rise in the instance,
drenching into the path unread that stays too late.

When the reconciled moment fades from the shore,
to leave the memories in solace evermore.

Lost to begin with

Lost it,
I didn't have it to begin with,
it did not exist within me.
it is not something that I can fathom.

Chantelle Lowe

faded by the cover of turmoil amid the shadows cast,
   in a fantasy trailing the lost dreams evermore.

Transitioning the role smothered under the weight of despise,
   withholding the flow through the mar of uncertainty,
   restricting all sense of self under repression of demise,
   inflicting a cacophony of envy into a lasting tragedy.

All waits for the fading hour to rise from an intrinsic trance,
   no more would it take hold to filter in the one left to stand,
   of all aspects of identity calling from a distance,
   breaking through in the finality to refuse the demand.

In a solitary pose that reconciled a vast entanglement,
seeping through the wounds that led to a false endearment.

Mixed dreams

Tranquillity reaches minds in an ever resounding peace,
culminating in a finite venture upon the stage,
yet the underlying value fails to cease,
even though the dying day begins to age.

An intrinsic event situates itself in the future rare,
though hidden from view as the time passes by,
cultivating the dreams mixed with envy to bear,
in the everlasting flow that gathers to tie.

The emanating rush of the tidal wave,
crashes upon the shore with a steady beat.

Mortal wound

For all that I have risen for,
in the days of young and old,
to rest upon my lap all cold.

For I have gone through yesteryear,
going forth through day and night,
the toll sits upon the morning light.

For I have seen the face of grief,
the long and unsteady stance,
holding in a moment's glance.

For I have heard the tragic toll,
sweeping still across the land,
caressing in the final command.

For I have felt the languid stare,

Chantelle Lowe

resisting from a vibrant age,
upon the distant external stage.

For in this moment of solitude,
filled with a final calm and grace,
life walks toward the dark embrace.

For all I know have gone before,
calling closer to time's open door,
the mortal wound forever more.

Moving remnants

To mark the score of integrity upon the shore,
where the intensity of emotion had taken place,
transitioning into the infinite form of before,
trailing in the enormity along the surface.

Capturing the presence in the midst of uncertainty,
through the darkness roaming inside the mind,
that caressed the soul as it fled into destiny,
in a faded hour of restoration to unwind.

Glimpsing the shallow ruins taking hold inside,
to sprawl throughout the furthest travel,
wrapping around the last glimmer to confide,
where few tread in the harshness to unravel.

Moving ever closer to the remnants of the past,
underneath the madness of the shadow cast.

Chantelle Lowe

Narrow night

Death has become me,
like the whispering narrowed night.
Nothing falls to sleeplessness,
as the rain it conquers everything.

Chantelle Lowe

No in between

Cover my soul when I am whole for there is no in between,
where sparrows go and others follow on the edge of what is seen,
a tragic course I must admit, which falters within the cascade,
a hidden truth that stays remit, in the burden of the final raid.

Chantelle Lowe

No mark

Killer, killer in the night,
roaming, dark and free.
Is it to bear such a sight,
when no harm can mark thee?

No more the dark carries

The time that remains undone I fear,
where the mortal eye crosses my path,
folding in the shadows that appear,
covered with apathy turned to wrath.

A glimpse into the future and dare,
where the past ruptures through the disgrace,
shattering the comfort that will bear,
fading with the distance formed in space.

The paths that sear upon the morrow,
collide with a peril reaching past,
the eternal struggle in the sorrow,
drenching into the terrain so vast.

A glance that shared the anguish and guilt,
yet parted way on a common thread,

Chantelle Lowe

long after the turmoil that built,
exacting a toll covered in dread.

The culmination of all events,
to carry the burden on the shore,
where the waves can wipe all that torments,
in the memories forever more.

A tragedy that glides through the night,
to wake the troubled mind from slumber,
in the shadows that cross into sight,
where no more the dark carries over.

The weeping of the eternal mind,
into the cavities that remind.

Chantelle Lowe

No patience

I hear destiny calling me.
It is a patience,
I seem to call,
as a feeling,
towards it.
It reaches out to me,
I have no patience.
All I see,
is today,
not tomorrow,
nor the future.

Chantelle Lowe

Not knowing

Invasion to know, interrogation to see,
corruption to find, propaganda to be.
Everything is clear in here,
clear beyond the sky.
It smells through the rafters,
clinging to the ties,
Not knowing the smooth transition,
between space.

Chantelle Lowe

Obelisk

I am the barren obelisk,
it twirls, it twirls, it spins.
So thorough does the dice roll,
it seeps through every gap.
Find me, find me,
oh do come and play.
For everyone is not at all,
for whom or what they seem.

In greyness and darkness
they all fly about.
Until one tires,
then they all fall down,
strewn across the grass.
Then skitter scatter, away they go,
safe into the night.

Oblivion

To bless the soul so dearly,
at an integral of time.
To perish to oblivion,
would be magnificent,
if it was wanted.
This apocalypse is seen as varied,
though it is not much.

Chantelle Lowe

On a small dream

This is my moment, I stand on the precipice of time,
looking down upon all that I have done.
For now I can stand alone,
leaving my past behind me,
yet grasping it in both hands.
Taking it with me in pride and grace,
for in this world I do not have long.
I hold my hand up high to reach the stars,
as I once did wishing, with one now in heaven, on a small dream.
I hold out all my fears for others here to see,
and the grief I have known as the future I do not fear.
Yet in darkness I will strive,
with shame and hurt now gone.
There is but one thing I have left undone in this world,
and now I let it fly up to the stars to reign free.

Chantelle Lowe

One desire

My poetry is my life,
my full heart of desires.
The only one which I possess.

Chantelle Lowe

One journey to trace

If not for me then when, in the shadows that mark the day,
if not for me then when, in the hours that mark dismay?
For all that is wrought before, each passing moment does define,
for all that is wrought before, in the presence of the devine.

No matter which way it went, the path continues to divide,
no matter which way it went, no other will confide.
For reaching in the in between, an eminent thought takes place,
for reaching in the in between, there is only one journey to trace.

Chantelle Lowe

One person

I am but one person.
What does one person
know about all the problems
of the world?
Very little.

One small act

A tragedy as yet unfolds in distrust,
for alliances are shed and left to rust,
in the wake of turmoil in the set,
scattering the unbreakable to forget.

Yet pieces of the whole remain,
leaving the mark of another stain,
trailing into the edge of undeniability,
where the sequence ponds for all to see.

Did anyone think it could be washed away,
to never set forth on another day?
When all it took was one small act,
unaware of the underlying impact.

Chantelle Lowe

On my own

The image imprints itself on the mind, damaging as it is.
My image was damaged before, not anything real,
now it is real, and I am not sure if I feel anything at all.
Often I ask myself why when I have not done wrong,
now I have and in some way I deserve it, but I am so used it.
So used to being blamed and having a bad reputation,
when doing nothing to deserve it.
Is it fair to live up to that, when so many others do the same,
and are still seen as little darlings.
I did not get that when I was.
It would be ironic if I was seen on the outside as I really was before,
being nice and polite let me down so badly, it gave me no friends at all.
People passed me by, not wanting to know me.
Perhaps if I took a little risk, I would make a few friends,
instead of being lonely on my own.

Chantelle Lowe

On the wave of regret

Simplicity wedges itself in through the turmoil,
taking with it the undisputed hand of grace,
with the flowing presence that does not recoil,
amid the ripples that carry along the surface.

Reaching for consistency in a time of subterfuge,
under the cover of darkness that hails down,
a restless anticipation where all take refuge,
where the water's depths take hold and drown.

For sorrows weep under the merging hollow tide,
wailing into the howling wind as it rips,
with a haste all too soon on a searing ride,
where eternity builds in the name of old until it tips.

Reaching for the soul as it caves within the fading hour,
to rest upon a wave of regret that dismantles the tower.

Chantelle Lowe

Other self

I see you in full height,
as a person of some means.
In the surroundings you are great,
but on your own you are nothing,
because you have no one to hold you up.
In your own atmosphere,
in your own solitude,
it will always creep,
your other.

Our mistakes

When time comes,
it will stay,
for good,
and conquer,
evil,
destruction,
humanity.
In due course,
it will,
wipe out our mistakes,
and heal our wrong.

In the daytime it will come,
soaring well above the damp ground,
to determine our position.

Chantelle Lowe

Over the landscape

Places none too common,
see my roaming eyes.
Over the landscape, hither yonder,
where none other than I do see,
a place to calm the squelching fire,
and brings back those to me.

Chantelle Lowe

Paralleled sadness

Tragedy, paralleled sadness,
covering the remainder of the day.
An opinion unsaid left in doubt.

Chantelle Lowe

Passing through

The queries of the mind open doors I cannot find,
through an approaching haze that wraps around a maze,
and all that is sort was what had been left behind,
marking the disparity said with flawless praise.

In the depths of the shrine that was not meant to be mine,
tracing uncertainty where the whole would not let it be,
masking a sorrow that overflowed by design,
when pity fled the hand that greeted all to see.

For seeking no more shall I wash upon the shore,
that graces along and all that remains is gone,
resting in a finality that spreads before,
an ensuing integration of the time whereon.

Passing through a devastation pulled from the past,
to entertain the universe until the last.

Chantelle Lowe

Path of intuition

It is not my question why,
it is not locked in time's eye.
Taken down the path of intuition.
The emblem of desire,
reeking forward.

Path of tragedy

If all hope were to wither away,
amid the dying of the final day.
It would take with it the oldest memory,
set into a path of tragedy.

The unseen time held in place,
when all is lost within the space,
unfolding to watch what was done,
when the eternal passage has yet begun.

A reminder of all left to be,
where there is no one left to see,
as the last moment breaks in the final hour,
leaving the seeping darkness to devour.

Chantelle Lowe

Piling in a mound

When whispers along the road mistook,
a little of every day,
there came a time when all was gone,
withering away.
Yet no higher thought,
did touch the ground,
when moments of nothing came by,
piling up in a mound.
Tripping over the words unsaid,
holding up the impasse,
for an uncertainty,
unravelling at the pass.

Predicament

Everyday I question myself,
over things which happened.
One of the hardest things is knowing that in reality,
there exists very few real answers,
very few if any.
The hardest thing is knowing that I was not to blame,
because then it means that others were at fault,
others who do not admit guilt.
It leaves me in a predicament,
because by admitting I was not to blame.
It alienates me from them.
They live their false reality and I cannot accept it.
When they find out I live in the truth,
they ignore me,
or scorn me angrily for disturbing their cosy world.
It does not matter to them that I hurt.

Chantelle Lowe

Pressure

It is a supplement only,
to turn in on yourself,
and expose the pressures which hold,
then release.

Chantelle Lowe

Presumptuous dream

Treasure the moments that come sporadically,
in the ease and grace of the words unsaid,
lifting the tumultuous thoughts of antiquity,
from the reaching desires that lie ahead.
If time were eternity it would not conquer all,
in the desperation of certainty when those close fall.

If the way ahead was determined forward,
every moment would count as though forever,
a presumptuous dream to walk toward,
when the only ties are left to sever.
In a world where redemption gives way to the grave,
and all the thoughts that aspire are left yet to pave.

A moment of solace reckons the hand of guilt,
covering the memory into the eternal flow,
pouring until the distorted weight does tilt,

Chantelle Lowe

with all the subtleties that let go.
Filling the tide that accumulates on the shore,
merging with the footsteps of long before.

Chantelle Lowe

Prism of uncertainty

The prism of uncertainty devours with every stride,
taking with it anonymity as the rain conquers all,
for every part of the journey takes a side,
where the only way forward is to fall.

Perhaps the path lies in uncertainty reaching for the ground,
an infinite number of recollections to disband,
when the traveller's way is no more found,
where the rising toll makes the final demand.

For the way ahead plagues the fading past,
wrapped in the dismay of the many,
gathering with it the judgement cast,
in the solitude of a vague uncertainty.

Chantelle Lowe

Quandary

It is to be great,
yet nothing at all?
When you see it, it comes forth,
into the space, into the time,
and no matter how far you go, you will always be here.

Chantelle Lowe

Reaping madness

Peaceful steps are but a tragedy waiting on the eternal stage,
an epiphany of regret mirrored in the turmoil ahead,
a place which turns to disarray in the faded image,
calling of a darker time in the mind left unsaid.

A recognition of the intrepid form riddled with uncertainty,
ebbing down into the imbuing flow teaming with a sadness,
a combination of the end of dreams trapped in ability,
covering the time towards the reaping of its madness.

A single thought clinging to the unfailing sign,
when lighter moments brought forward an endearing dawn,
washed away by a tumultuous line,
in a careless moment leaving all forlorn.

Writhing through an insidious demise,
before stepping forward to again rise.

Redeeming factor

Deliberately squandering the truth,
opening the door to humiliation,
grasping for air in the unforeseen.
Placing my will, as I have placed before,
into the redeeming factor.
Collaborating the essential time,
with wealth and fascination.

Chantelle Lowe

Reeling

Transmission of the intersection of time wrapping forward,
a reminder of the flow into identity,
reeling away the essence.

Chantelle Lowe

Rejection

Culmination of fear, degradation,
evolving, taking time.
Rejection, not knowing.
Take, take away.

Chantelle Lowe

Remnant for which I mourn

For the coming of the dawn shall take me,
from this time to another when all is lost,
yet no more will the path let it be,
when to enter throughout fulfils a cost.

For uncertainty follows where others tread,
and no guidance exists in the final wedge,
where the silence gathers with the unsaid,
to part as one upon the resulting ledge.

Yet the path remains a treacherous one,
that comes and goes in the waking hour,
to pull apart the dream and hopes hard won,
and capture within its claws to devour.

For no mark shall see me at the door,
in the waking light creasing above the hill,

Chantelle Lowe

where shadows march along the floor,
culminating to the place where I am still.

A memory forsaken in a taunted image,
recollecting all that has been and past,
for darkness weeps where others pillage,
a stain unwary in the stance long cast.

For no creeping light from above the dawn,
will take the remnant pain for which I mourn.

Chantelle Lowe

Replacement

The goal of the situation was to take away
what had been harmful,
and replace it with something kind,
something adorable and complex.

Chantelle Lowe

Rhythmless tide

The time that passed this transition was immense,
calling forth on a rhythmless tide.
The feeling of trying to find what was lost,
something that went away unnoticed,
and now I do not know it.
A fathomless pit of information,
but do I need it?
I sign, not knowing
whether going forward
is worse than going backward.

Chantelle Lowe

Rippling away

Courage, the determining factor rippling away at the seams,
calling upon the fortitude that comes with restitution,
the untimely manner that seeps through the thoughts of those it deems,
an unwavering ideal explicit in its attempts of revolution.

Chantelle Lowe

Rising from burden

The unexpected intrusion of a gaze,
the epitome swept up in the haze,
circling the turmoil yet unsaid,
born into the pages still unread.

In the light that washes away the goal,
in the remainder of the damage from the toll,
creeping along the edges that begin to fray,
amid the rapid hour that fades away.

When the tears flow in abundance,
when all that turns stops in a trance,
the calm will enter in from the storm,
awaiting tranquillity in its form.

For a hope that rises out of burden,
to spread along the path well trodden.

Chantelle Lowe

Roads that intertwine

The culmination of the day,
plays in every way,
down my fingertips and down my spine,
as the essence of time goes by.
An intercepting thought on the roads that intertwine,
determining the damage wrought with a resounding heavy sigh.
An intrepidation of the time brought,
from an internal path of encumbrance,
when all the memories that have been sought,
sway upon the breeze in a solemn dance.

Chantelle Lowe

Rupturing the flow

Changing the time that ran away from destiny,
into the shadows that held a glimpse from behind,
when the one portrait that mattered was certainty,
curled up in the flame in the edge of the mind.

Besieged in the treachery with a resolution,
that undertakes the integrity of being,
in the demise that captures anticipation,
when the lost return upon the imagining.

Reaching for the edges that seep out underneath,
inspiring through turmoil from the pressure built,
under the immensity of the strain beneath,
when the angle that severs time begins to tilt.

Rupturing the even flow ingrained from within,
to absorb into the intensity therein.

Rustling leaves

Unravelling like the winds of time,
blowing on the breeze.
It came to me one fine spring day,
rustling through the leaves.
A small chill crept inside,
through the fabric of my clothes.
Part of me wanted to hide,
cover up and doze.

Chantelle Lowe

Sadness overwhelmed

I have an overwhelming sadness,
so deep inside me,
it is hard to keep.

Same place

Do you only think or do you see,
where I am and where I be?
If I were over there,
would you stare?
Or keep a blind eye,
to where I am to die?
Sitting over in the corner,
do you feel a little warmer?
Take thee,
leave me.
When I leave you follow,
and when you leave I go,
far away,
never stay,
in the same place,
you and I will pace.
Though never shall we meet,

Chantelle Lowe

for different times they do not greet.

Chantelle Lowe

Seek and find

Seek, and you shall find,
the same state of mind,
which appears out of sight,
covered away in the night.

Chantelle Lowe

Shallow fall

It kills yet does not seep,
through my heart and grace.
I have come yet so far,
to turn, then stay again.
The cushion of the fall,
is but a shallow one,
with a shallow grave to mark it.

Chantelle Lowe

Shall strike

When the light shall strike
for let be the night.

For the lady in white
will be in the right,

and nobody will be in dispute.

Chantelle Lowe

Sharpness felt

As I crossed the road,
on my palm the sharpness felt.
It was warm with the heat,
and did neither cut my hand,
nor help heal what had been, and lost.

Chantelle Lowe

Shell of time

To see the dim source,
catalyse with the stiff air.
All the peace,
as it shifts, miraculously,
in the shell of time.
Then wavers,
to fall, ever so slowly,
on the parachute of time.

Chantelle Lowe

Shoulder of time

This crime is unforgivable,
this mercy for all to see.
In name and glory,
upon the shoulder of time.

Chantelle Lowe

Slumber

To slumber, to sombre,
to an adequate,
of despise.
In attempt,
of vacillation,
to repose,
of reconcile.
In the ever me,
of pity,
does fall,
like antipathy,
to unstrangle,
the innocent,
in reconciliation,
of unimportance.
In ever reeling,
whine,

Chantelle Lowe

of anger,
split on sadness.
Is always forthcoming,
in tranquillity,
of the soul.

Chantelle Lowe

Solace with intention

Tragedy plays a role deep in the mind,
where colours flare into transition.
Filtering into the flowing waters to find,
a resting solace filled with intention.

Tracing uncertainty in its path to the end,
culminating into restitution for the land,
when we cannot see what lies around the bend,
while breaking through the past to make a stand.

Chantelle Lowe

Solid page

Here I sit and here I stay,
writing in my little way,
creeping, crawling from the pen,
to the solid page below.

Chantelle Lowe

Something heard

Then, in the distance,
I heard something being shouted over the shadows.
In my direction it came,
filling my heart and soul.

Chantelle Lowe

Something surreal

Time to combat reality,
with the sense that it has joined,
the world again.
For a while it was misplaced.
Taken on a sojourn,
not knowing where to turn.
It left me a while,
in something surreal.
Untuned to the life I have.
I let it flitter a little while,
as things became unknown,
but all that time,
it was with me,
laying dormant in my mind.
For in the outside world,
things were bleak,
making it easy to be let down.

Chantelle Lowe

I knew all the while,
I had to be somewhere else,
to cope with reality.

Chantelle Lowe

Sorrows underneath

No greater mind as I desire,
in name or other things,
for walk away and feel the fire,
and see what one task brings.

For the way ahead rests softer still,
as the dawn makes way anew,
an eternal gathering along the hill,
where stars fade across the hue.

If I were to walk to the clear blue sky,
with the haste of the breeze along the way,
and the sun's rays warm up high,
there would be no greater day.

Calming the sorrows underneath,
as the earth moves me forward from beneath.

Chantelle Lowe

Soul searching

Colours blow together in the eternal disarray,
a fathomless pit of soul searching
when the darkness finds a way,
and the path remains far reaching.

Chantelle Lowe

Still I do not see

Time is but of the essence,
I am who I am made to be.
All is not as it was,
and I wish to be it.
Take my hand across the region of time,
and hold it steady.
Can you see it falling,
down to instability?
I place my will into my own,
and still I do not see.

Chantelle Lowe

Stop them

I try to stop them,
I hold them back,
I see in time,
I was right.

When I look down,
when they crumble,
when I smile at their misery,
when their thoughts do not reach mine.

That is when I fly free,
that is my final destination,
that which I accomplish,
that what I seek.

Through their fire I hear their displeasure,
through which I laugh with glee,

Chantelle Lowe

through my eyes for which I see,
through my satisfaction.

Strength to stand

Into the torment the fantasy hides,
away from prying eyes with a burden,
that reaches far beyond the rising tides,
swallowing humility forbidden.

Covering the broken souls in demise,
purging in the fallout reaching on high,
when in the sorrows the details rise,
catching on a trance that quells to defy.

For when the shadows are lost to amend,
the image that remains under the strain,
to beckon to the undeserving end,
emanating from the hollows of pain.

That creep upon the surface that repels,
within the infernal mind long after,

Chantelle Lowe

the grasping of uncertainty dispels,
into the flow that holds the disaster.

In the crumbling pieces that devour,
the enormity of the task at hand,
falling away to glimpse the last hour,
to take defeat and hold the strength to stand.

Chantelle Lowe

Sweeping past

If sweeping past you see me then,
know that I am gone,
If walking down the pathway,
you look for me,
know that I had been there.
If travelling along the open road,
know that I am not behind you.
If glancing around the vacant room,
know that this is not my home.

Chantelle Lowe

Take away the harm

Take away all the harm,
send it away without warning.
Take it to a barren place,
lacking of life and other things.
May it go away,
from this place and leave us behind.

Chantelle Lowe

Taking hold

Culmination of fear,
taking hold.
Repetition, premonition,
cultivating the world.

Tangled in the fray

Opportunity will float on the dawn,
in an array of fleeting colours,
covering the essence as once it stood,
tangled in the fray of other matters.

It will seep across the open door,
filling vibrant dreams with goals,
wrapping around a moment's thought,
as the turmoil of future calls.

The happen stance of a fleeting path,
leading through the unseen gains,
bringing with it the swaying loops,
that flood across the hopes and pains.

To travel the moment of uncertainty,
and hold onto a glimpse of clarity.

Chantelle Lowe

Task of ambition

In the term of uncertainty,
the inevitable happens.
In a recurring structure,
to implicate the other form.
In the gratifying task,
of ambition.
In coupling the serenity
of the complex issue,
in time will for hold.

Chantelle Lowe

Tethered breeze

The mists of time echoed an uneven past,
where hollows of memories lay,
taking away the shadows cast,
holding tight the fragile day.

The ever rolling stretch of riverbed,
glimpsing upon the tethered breeze,
with a welcome relief ahead,
while setting the mood at ease.

For on the warmth of the sun held high,
brought a simple elegant air,
where golden rays reach for the sky,
in the weather sure and fair.

A fine day spread across the land,
for all to admire as they stand.

Chantelle Lowe

The concept of the legacy

In the harshest hour before the dawn when the moon takes form,
out of darkness and insanity rises the past of many long years,
it filters through the time reaching out amidst a raging storm,
for beneath the layers of mistrust and sorcery it appears.

Growing in the turmoil comes a messenger born in the form a child,
deep in the heart of sorcery breaks free hard into the open fray,
for what has been unleashed in the treachery must be reconciled,
in the heart of a girl lay the oldest sorcery rising in the light of day.

For what was and what shall be, will be rewritten in the land of old,
and what lay beneath the surface reawakens in a world of despair,
the dying hand of friendship fulfils the story as once was told,
with the whispering wind as it seeps through the sky with an heir.

What lay forgotten has risen as the flame grows ever higher,
for the child of sorcery strides from the shadows and into the raging fire.

The concept of the mark

Amid infernal flames of trepidation wrapped in frame,
emerge the courage sort in hidden refuge,
from the fractured will that transpires the game,
born in wretched darkness and deluge.

For the sorrows filter through those who remain,
culminating a dangerous choice to bear,
under the insidious pressure to refrain,
and the shattering of hope left to despair.

In the treasured moment to caress the land,
all withered and worn in the heat of rage,
washes away the last hesitation to stand,
where all that is and was marks the stage.

A force unreckoned in the ultimate glory,
laying the way to forgiveness of an untold story.

Chantelle Lowe

The coming of night

The shadow of the night,
shall thrive to kill,
everything,
shall be its victim.

Chantelle Lowe

The day flourishes

Fair roses mired by the ground's earth,
breaking through the coil of dismay,
to spread beauty for all it is worth,
under the ever watchful sun's ray.

No sooner than the warmth is felt,
upon the finer day that flourishes out,
there craves a desire in what was dealt,
to make amends where there was doubt.

For in the unfurled petals to the sun,
where the fragrant breeze descends,
there lies much more work to be done,
than the time given to make amends.

Where shadows falter on this fine day,
and the birds that visit go about their way.

The deepest thoughts

Treasure of the soul the deepest thoughts so rare,
when all know the toll of a future held so fair,
yet the way ahead struggles deep within the mind,
making a source of light through the darkness hard to find.

Simplicity calls of sweeter times in hope and joy,
when the memory of pleasant things become null and void,
an arbitrary question lies on tender lips,
not wanting to break the spell until the moment tips.

For all the courage in the final waking hour,
it yells and screams when all around turns sour,
though not a waking thought it creeps in through the day,
suggesting sorrowful matters others hold at bay.

It caresses a different time, a moment between you and I,
when all was well upon the surface going by,

Chantelle Lowe

until the dawn broke with the glowing sun,
and the image faded in the damage done.

The idea lingers

Travesty makes the final call amid the gloom,
when the trust fades in the weakened grasp,
and the turmoil waits for no one in the doom,
of an eternal voice through a grating rasp.

The idea lingers yet to grow old,
in a place ravaged by the shadows cast,
and those who band are yet to be told,
when the winds of change carry the past.

If I let go I could take it with ease,
a steady restful giant held in disguise,
when there is no one left to appease,
and the only path ahead will rise.

For all that I have treasured will lead away,
and only the steadfast on the journey will stay.

Chantelle Lowe

The mind that is

What is all this coming to?
When no one hears what is,
in the terrible mind that is.

The path of integrity

Transparency takes away the image that shatters all,
when the world turns and the lights dim,
clouds swirl in as the battered leaves fall,
and the path ahead darkens as the way turns grim.

Is it the journey that narrows as time grows thin,
or the filtering of chaos through the storm,
a transient notion that raises from within,
at a stage when the final mark takes form?

Resolute is the decision of finality seeping past,
as the silence grows after all discretions are done,
shaping the memories of the mind from shadows cast,
when the path is only wide enough for one.

Taking the turmoil that creeps through reality,
with a truth foretold long before the light of day,

Chantelle Lowe

caressing the future that remains solitary,
through the fixations that imprison the way.

For the darkness grows in the longing of the dawn,
unravelling lost hopes with every passing stride,
when so many moments trickle away forlorn,
resting on the avalanche of whispers to confide.

If there were a reason to sweep across the journey,
an explanation of certainty amid the mess,
it would fade into the waves that meld into the sea,
and lose grip under the multitude of stress.

Albeit a short moment along the path to integrity,
plummeting into the darkest withered place,
a shallow whimper in the face of all uncertainty,
where the wind sweeps away every trace.

If I had known it was meant for me,
would I have turned away from all the darkness?
When the path ahead I do not see,
through the mountains of so much sadness.

Perhaps another time the path will guide,

Chantelle Lowe

yet on my journey the memories seep,
through the harrowing storm to the other side,
where the path leads to all I will safely keep.

For travelling through the storm I go,
knowing the final cost that is to stay,
from all the harm that had to flow,
before the resolution made the way.

Every step forward takes away the pain,
clinging through the shadows cast,
a moment held in dignity to remain,
reaching for the journey to the last.

A cost so deep that hope seeps through,
weighing on the path for the final cue.

Chantelle Lowe

The path that leads

Mired in the place I went,
mired in the messages sent,
eclipsing the steps left behind,
eclipsing the toll to remind,
replacing the subtle facade,
replacing the fake promenade.

Turning from the pages swept,
turning from the moments wept,
embracing in the fallen haze,
embracing in the unmarked maze,
standing on the path that leads,
standing on the crest of deeds.

Chantelle Lowe

The path turned

Dancing up the hallways of an unframed mind,
when the way is distant through the clouds ahead,
'Go this way,' you said and I answered in kind.
seeing the waters seep along as we fled.

Yet all the paths turned to one,
as the cold cradled the frail heart,
racing in waves as the work was undone,
in a trail making its way around to the start.

For as the clouds set in, darkening the sky,
the raging torrent caressed the uneven ground,
a turbulent sway beckoned from up high,
as each step drew the mud from around.

For in the darkness as the rain drenched through,
the fog lifted and the end came into view.

Chantelle Lowe

The real me

In my place,
I see the world through catastrophe,
crippling everything in sight.
It comforts me,
to know that others are weak,
and can be defeated,
and in my place I will stand.
Strong as any other,
until I fall and am crushed,
heavily, deeply,
in upon myself,
and will see a new me,
the real me.

Chantelle Lowe

The unresolved

The fluid motion that saunters in,
to find the darkness swirling around,
the edges of eternity pin,
into the crevasses underground.

Wrapping the frame that lingers inside,
where the mind wanders the unresolved,
that torments in the ways that do abide,
when searching for a longing dissolved.

Into the trenches of time make way,
the subtlety that remains behind,
where the past drenches holding at bay,
the myriad of flaws in the mind.

For no path can shatter lasting doubt,
hidden in the coils that hold grace,

Chantelle Lowe

in a refuge left broken throughout,
forsaking the image to surface.

In the weathered hand that cradles time,
merging sanctity with turmoil,
to create an elegance sublime,
amid the perpetual toil.

Where distant shadows dwell to lay claim,
to the mirage that sweeps across land,
persevering in front of the blame,
that curls its way into the demand.

When all that weeps draws away to fade,
sinking into the enormity,
from pressure of the toll to be paid,
in the final hour of certainty.

When the scars that remain to defy,
the rumours that change the lasting cost,
reminiscent of the past gone by,
sweeping into an aftermath lost.

To the rows of deceit and dismay,

Chantelle Lowe

covering ground in perpetuity,
with incessant matters to decay,
through the hallmark of eternity.

Through the essence

Is fate not forgiveness in the throws of the moment,
wishing everything away in the turmoil of regret,
a second thought enamoured inside the torment,
leaving but a glimpse in the absence to let?

Does a single moment stop in the distance,
between the ravages that seep into the mind,
spiralling into the incessant storm at a glance,
where all but who remains is there to find?

And yet the temper flares with a memory,
lingering into the distant stare of willingness,
for time it gathers speed in all the uncertainty,
filtering into the uneven flow of unworthiness.

Descending into uncharted debris of the sublime,
through the essence that covers the hallmark of time.

Chantelle Lowe

Tied with destiny

The time runs through my veins as any other,
a tragedy lying in wait from uncertainty,
unfolding as the crowd begins to gather,
when the real toll is tied with destiny.

The transition into the path that determines the way,
when the follower leads no more through the haze,
and the darkness swirls amid the decay,
foreshadowing the tremors sweeping through the maze.

When all is lost and fallen into the dust,
there is a decision that weighs upon the mind,
as hope fades along with the trust,
and the result is what is left to find.

Chantelle Lowe

Time draped in harshness

To run the gauntlet into the depths of despair,
when all that matters has gone through the air,
diving into the storm that awaits from the blast,
purging the hope from those holding out last.

For no matter which way the bitterness is said,
it still shatters the dreams that remain unread,
tossing into the darkness an unwillingness led,
where the cold reaches all that need to be fed.

In a time draped in harshness with a pity all hollow,
breaking into the turmoil for the foolhardy to follow,
yet the sway that drives through into the harshest bend,
does nothing to play down the sorrow and amend.

For time heals some wounds more than others felt,
when the past emerges to show the hand dealt,

Chantelle Lowe

no more will the pain rise with the sense of agony,
to pilfer the remnants blown to the wind in pity.

On the journey that favoured no more than the other,
bringing an intensity to dwell and then smother,
each step berated the last in shameful recognition,
where hope faded under the shadow cast in depletion.

No reckoning would prolong the time that is left,
leaving the whole drama with the people bereft.

Chantelle Lowe

Time of disbelief

The life which has gone before,
sees the place not yet born.
Of hope beyond relief,
in a time of disbelief.

Chantelle Lowe

Time to regret

A tumultuous time of regret,
pulled down by a thought so shallow.
So cold and grey it covers the edges of all eternity,
to blend into the unwavering seams.

A foreshadowing of the uneven whole,
glimmering in a distant wallow.
Yet the saddest of all thoughts still remains,
glimpsing up at an unforeseen light.

Taking away thought and shadow,
in a timely yet fair embrace.

Chantelle Lowe

To be without

Epitome of the soul,
is to be without.
Without everything in life,
which holds us together.
Without autonomy.

Chantelle Lowe

To imagination

Take yourself up out of the world of the real,
and down into the world of imagination.
Ascending to a higher place,
descending to the inner space.

Chantelle Lowe

To know

How can I conquer,
what I have come for?
When I have yet,
to know what it is?

Chantelle Lowe

Toll of integrity

Death is the toll of integrity,
to be what is not,
and induce what is.

Chantelle Lowe

To ruin

You ruin my life,
you ruin my hatred,
you ruin my love.

Chantelle Lowe

Tragedy unravels

For I have travelled the seas abound,
lifting the tides eternal pace,
into the raging storms aground,
where each passing step leaves a trace.

For I can walk the timeless floor,
holding pages of eternity in hand,
towards the long held open door,
where tragedy unravels into sand.

Trapped in betrayal

Trapped in the ultimate betrayal of trust,
where shadows linger in the dark regret,
for the way ahead will be as it must,
when the conjurer would rather I forget.

A turmoil raging between anger and shock,
from an untimely reminder of cruelty at hand,
bestowed in malevolence as though to mock,
the sincerity behind a genuine demand.

Yet know it not upon the shore of time,
the tranquillity hides a deeper mind,
rustling amid the vast array of rhyme,
a culmination of restitution does find.

The clueless of anonymity that kept so many before,
has laid bare the disingenuity at the holder's door.

Chantelle Lowe

Travesty

Travesty, travesty, turn around,
travesty, travesty, touch the ground,
caress the earth for which we have seen,
take to this world as though we have been.
For all among us go which way and that,
placing the burden onto the mat.

Travesty, travesty, where are you found,
travesty, travesty, when there is no sound?
Take my hand and we'll run through the night,
listening through the gaps that hold everything tight.
For there is no greater place to hold you and I,
when all the world crumbles as others go by.

Chantelle Lowe

Treachery seeping through

Disinterest,
disintegration into eternity,
abomination,
absolution of recognition,
and then came the storm,
dripping down.
Turmoil begets with turmoil,
ascension and relief,
juxtaposed in time.
A hanging thread,
predominantly mine,
of something left unsaid,
but can I not be,
for all eternity?
When the raging storm seeks refuge.
An enigmatic light,
resting in the dawn,

Chantelle Lowe

a troubled soul taking plight,
in the treachery seeping through.
Is all as it was,
when the way ahead is blocked?
Was it meant to be,
in the searing eternal flame of hope?
A tragedy yet unfurled,
to take the dice as it twirled,
for all the time that yet has been.

Chantelle Lowe

Troubled path

A discouragement sits at my door,
not wanting to be let in.
A stranger not knowing if there is more,
from the hurt filled within.

A swaying hand to see the light,
a shadow cast in doubt.
No one close to hold me tight,
when calm is nowhere about.

A troubled path I do not seek,
though some may see it so.
A glimpse ahead of something bleak,
holding the overflow.

Yet the hand that reaches is not mine,
and as time passes I will hold the line.

Chantelle Lowe

Unacceptance

In a world of unacceptance,
I reach forward,
I hear my name called,
but I am not accepted.
Instead I find myself,
in a whole new plane of existence.
Something hardened through experience,
to the final destination.

Chantelle Lowe

Uncommon means

Tragedy strikes in an uncommon means upon the morrow,
claiming the unready that traverse the simplest ground,
yet the time has gone for those to follow,
when there is no more to place around.

Chantelle Lowe

Undefined layer

Reflection correlates with the eternity of transition,
culminating in an undefined layer seeping through the many,
even though the turmoil provides ammunition,
along the hours that pass into infinity.

Chantelle Lowe

Underlying fold

Rest assured by no means possible,
left in an ugly state,
an unfathomable question reaching forward,
asked for all too late.

A substantial means of reckoning,
in a careless fragile hold,
a stiffening of retribution felt,
in an underlying fold.

Though not seen by way of tragedy,
accruing with desire,
a whim long felt in the aftermath,
from the harshness of the fire.

A hand that swept the tears away,
to hold resolute and not give sway.

Underneath the strain

For the figure sees no more through the open door,
when the rain quells the empty storm anew,
glistening in the light that fades even more,
while the tragedy is known to but a few.

Passing away into the fabric of time lost,
in the hour dire to those who remain,
from distant shores all the same within the cost,
to seek and restore a lost demise to refrain.

A plight torn from the disarray seeping forward,
to churn through the dismay clinging to what was gone,
when the ripples seeped from the edge moving toward,
a moment captured in a silence trapped upon.

While uncertainty lingered in a cold fate,
where the whispers shattered a solace to endure,

Chantelle Lowe

with the reckoning taking form in the debate,
saturating a hold that cowered from the pure.

Risen to enormity when the path crumbles,
parting for the turmoil to erase the task,
in the reaches that sooth when what remains tumbles,
from the worn and fragile fixture of the mask.

Eclipsing duty and refuge that lies in wait,
in the myriad of emotions holding fast,
before the picture falls to flow and saturate,
into an abyss wrapped around a shadow cast.

For the time that spreads across an unrivalled pain,
brings with it the turmoil underneath the strain.

Chantelle Lowe

Uneasiness

Soon will come a day of uneasiness,
it will shatter all hope,
and dispel all fears.
I want you to realise,
that I am not one,
but many, who have put faith in me.

Chantelle Lowe

Unhelpful wish

Is there anything at all which could stop,
an unknown time and place.
As it seeps out of the corners of hope and despair,
to pull at the edges of the ice cold fragments,
which twist and turn the fated soul to pieces.
It is a time for an unhelpful wish to see another night,
when the soul wakes, let free by the day's passing turn.
I climbed the tree of hope, to see what I could find,
and found nothing.
In the distant place where I stayed,
it curled up to the sky.
When there was no place to hide its taunting eyes,
it had found its peace,
but I had not found mine.

Unintentional remnants

If I were to emerge from the thought whole,
would it seep into the everlasting flow?
Would it travel down the path of time,
gathering the remnants left to grow?

Capturing moments drifting through the space,
the tiny flecks as they swirl outward,
spiralling into the rising dawn,
as the sun's eternal rays ebb toward.

The light breeze whisks away uncertainty,
following the warmth ebbing into the day,
washing the doubts into memory,
as the ever rising clouds sway.

In every thought the moment plagues the mind,
yet the resolution remains elusive to find.

Chantelle Lowe

Unknown quantity

To destroy a feeling,
of unknown quantity,
Is to discriminate,
against the idea.

Chantelle Lowe

Unmarked terrain

Affirmation, confirmation of a whole,
reflective of society,
contributing nothing.
Where is the awareness,
the awareness of a whole?
In the dying days of integrity,
gripping the soul.
Leaking onto unmarked terrain,
giving rise to its present forms.

Chantelle Lowe

Untimely thought

If not for me, then for you,
although it may be too late to,
when all the covers are laid bare,
where all around we can stare.

Yet it is not made for one,
in this world when it is done,
gathering with it speed,
under the all mighty deed.

And yet there is no despair,
in the judgement laid unfair,
for no ascribing can deter,
the untimely thought after.

Yet when all has been said,
the damage will remain unread.

Chantelle Lowe

Waiting patiently

In the ebony room I sit,
waiting patiently,
here the wind blows all day,
never calming down.

War

Bang!
Shall fall a thousand swords
never to be used again.
Bang!
Will go the shiny ice
upon the crystal cup.
Dead!
Will be the souls of many
that lay to rest.
Dead!
Shall lay a thousand great minds
that stood together as one.
Gone!
The glory shattered
never to return.
Not!
Shall they try again

Chantelle Lowe

**but in another time
it will always continue.**

Chantelle Lowe

Way assured

Rest assured this is the way ahead.
Though I have not seen it before,
I am certain of what it has become.
In my own futile way,
I am sure of what I must do next.

Chantelle Lowe

Way vve fall

As to one,
to one and all.
Sit down,
and the way we fall.

Chantelle Lowe

What has been wrought

To see what has been wrought,
in all that has begun.
Into this little world,
of all the molten shame.

When darkness calls

For the darkness that carries through the moment,
for all the thoughts that drove to eternity,
when the path remained unfinished and unspent,
along a trail that filtered the past into reality.

For a memory that swept away a sense of reason,
for all the ground that slipped away in a cold motion,
when the journey was marred by every season,
along the travels that took their toll in the commotion.

For a time when all hope turned the other way,
for all the effort that burdened the initial fall,
when the devastation crept through every day,
along the retribution with the final call.

Among the myriad of dreams left to wait,
when the burden of the toll did not abate.

Chantelle Lowe

When no one hears

No hope holds the dawn of tomorrow,
I can find no way out.
All is as nothing,
when no one is seen.
Can nothing be apart,
when no one hears.

Chantelle Lowe

When sadness reappears

For eternity waits in the darkness to follow,
escaping from the cataclysm that drenched the soul,
taking its place on the fringe of intensity,
where the mind carries the fortunate from below,
embracing the warmth that encapsulates the whole,
while the tragedy flowed from the earth to be.

For the day that turned to dust in the shadow's hold,
breaking under the immensity born in fate,
surpassing through the harshest imagination,
revelling in the depredation to behold,
when all the stories are left vanquished all too late,
past the unending turmoil of frustration.

For the shadow that grazes the uneven hand,
tells a history long after the stain disappears,
from a thunderous awakening that dispels,

Chantelle Lowe

the tragedy that wraps itself around the land,
when in the duration takes form and reappears,
to soften the ever reaching sadness that dwells.

Chantelle Lowe

When the final hand moves

For everything shall not be the same,
if I hold on for a moment in despair,
a tragedy in all but name,
while trickling into the air.

A sacrifice where all do tread,
reaching for the hope of dawn,
an unseen path that lies ahead,
and a heavy price yet born.

For in the thick of treachery,
weighs the darkest thought,
creasing through the scenery,
of all the turmoil that has been brought.

A time away on the road to nothing,
has delayed the treasures of a wayward mind,

Chantelle Lowe

cutting through the intensity it will bring,
lasting upon the many paths that bind.

Singeing away the army of regret,
amidst the timeless thunderous rain,
for here there are no warriors yet,
and still no one to remain.

In the reaper's way lies dread,
where few will travel onward,
a complexity left unsaid,
when the final hand moves forward.

A knowledge taken to the changing tide,
where shadows fade by either side.

Chantelle Lowe

Where others fear

Turmoil and disbelief wrap around the spire,
a culmination of time and waiting,
when all the past events transpire,
emanating from years of contemplating.

For the moment that left so long ago,
a fleeting glance of what could have been,
winding itself through the elegant flow,
with a patience in a foreshadowed scene.

Striving forward in the reluctance that followed,
a parting of ways before the dawn covers the soul,
a tragedy yet to unfold in a memory owed,
when the way ahead is left unwhole.

No one will call when the time is near,
for alone I tread where others fear.

Chantelle Lowe

Where reasons fade

The story that finishes many times,
reaching for the untold hand,
a whisper away from all that chimes,
sweeping through the wind swept land.

For not all tales end in woe,
traversing the hilltops along the sky,
where all who struggle go,
and the caress of time goes fleeting by.

A thousand reasons fade away,
among the encumbering tide,
following the whispering along the bay,
where restless souls confide.

A peace that becomes eternity,
in the realm of all uncertainty.

Chantelle Lowe

Whirling in a storm

A torrent of rain whirling in the storm of the mind,
where it all washes away into the distant form,
the culmination of a tragedy left behind,
when the last remaining hope is loath to transform.

Warmth is swept away underneath the stars,
where the breeze carries the sounds along,
yet silence follows the steady wall that bars,
in the space that surpasses the buffer holding strong.

An eternity reaches the weary hand that lays to rest,
a time that spreads before the dawn breaks through,
eclipsing the ground and uncertainty at the crest,
where the sun shadows over the land in view.

For no more will the doubt pour into sadness,
as the day grows old in the constant stream,

Chantelle Lowe

glimpsing a whirlwind of memories and madness,
encapsulated in a time buried in a dream.

Yet the harshness carries on long past the shadow,
where the wilting flow holds in a distant breeze,
taunting in a faint recognition I dare not follow,
when the path trails into an unsteady ease.

There takes the pain crumbling along the journey,
a haunting grief that sinks into my very being,
from the tilt of fate that passed through reality,
fading in the darkest thought in the midst of breaking.

Where the eternal wait beckons underneath the sky,
in a stream of consciousness that weighs up high.

Chantelle Lowe

Whirling time

Player, player in the dark,
what eternal place to spark?
A fleeting glance in the mortal eye,
to glimpse the memory holding by.
If I were to mark the ever whirling time,
it would see fit to rise sublime.
For as the player throws the dart,
no keener eye views the art.
No grace or sorrow strays from play,
when all who know make them pay.

Chantelle Lowe

Would it shatter?

If I were to take it all away would it shatter?
If I were to destroy it all would it scatter?
If I were to call out to the stars above would it matter?

Chantelle Lowe

Wretchedness

Topple into the dismay that reeks in retrospect,
drenching down into wretchedness that smothers,
the dishevelled grotesqueness that took away its aspect,
to stand away from intensity that seeps and covers.

Chantelle Lowe

Writhing in the moment

For I have seen the road ahead,
waiting in the gallows of a sunken ledge,
writhing in a moment holding fast and stead,
when the sorrows past make the pledge.
For I have wallowed in times so offbeat,
searing into a slow and unrelenting heat.

Chantelle Lowe

Yet to be remedied

Carrying through on promises perceived by individuals,
a lesson unlearned, yet remedied.
Touching the tip of the iceberg,
not wanting to look back.
I reach out, I have nothing,
I give so much, I try my hardest,
yet I receive nothing.
I try beyond my hardest,
yet still nothing.
As a young girl I had the confidence,
which was quickly beaten out of me.
Instead I have been installed with someone else's programme,
and I cannot get rid of it.

Chantelle Lowe

Your shoulders

I want to stop, stop everything.
Stop what has been happening,
stop while you can,
it doesn't mean anything.
Take me with you,
place it on your shoulders.

Chantelle Lowe

Your turn

When the tides
turn,
it will be your
turn.

www.ingramcontent.com/pod-product-compliance
Lightning Source LLC
Chambersburg PA
CBHW051207290426
44109CB00021B/2375